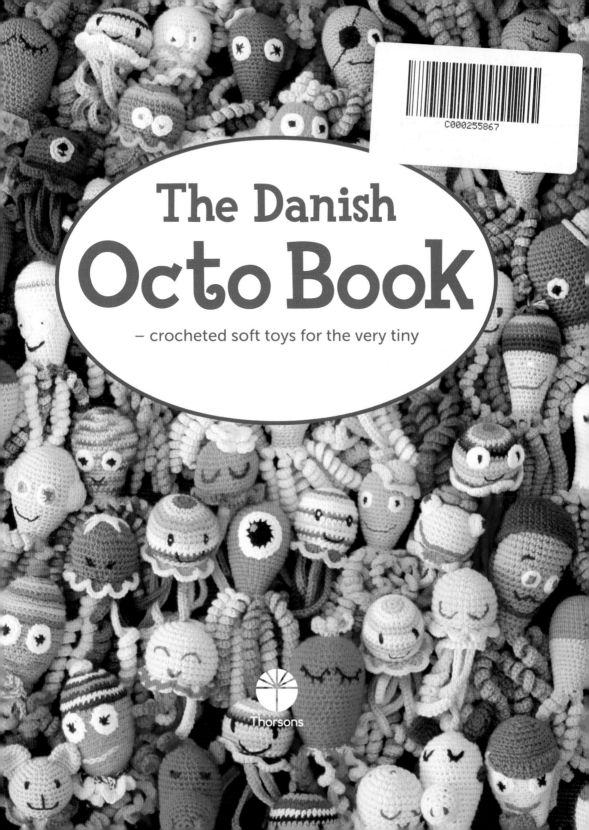

The Danish
Octo Book

– crocheted soft toys for the very tiny

Thorsons

Foreword

An Octo is a small, colourful crocheted or knitted octopus. An Octo can give comfort and security to a newborn baby, perhaps because its long tentacles are reminiscent of mum's umbilical cord. Normally, Octos are given to premature babies on neonatal wards across Denmark. They are made and collected in large numbers by the Danish Octo Project (Spruttegruppen). They are, of course, suitable for all little ones – both newborns and older kids alike – and now you too can bring a child happiness by making and decorating your own Octo. Inside, you will find instructions showing you how to make both the crocheted and knitted versions, as well as the cutest little jellyfish. Just like the Octos, the jellyfish have tentacles that are perfect for snuggling up to and tugging on. This book also contains instructions for decorations and ideas on how to give your Octos their own unique personalities. If you've never crocheted before, this book is a crochet school that will show you how. Not only that, the book will tell you a bit about what the Octo club does, and how to get involved if you want to donate Octos. These lovely little toys really aren't hard to make, so make yourself comfortable and let's get started!

The Danish Octo Project

The group was founded in 2013, and today the Octos it collects are distributed to every neonatal unit in Denmark and Greenland. It all started with one squid-obsessed dad whose daughter was born premature, and who then turned to a crochet blogger to ask whether she might be able to create a little squid for his daughter.

In the hospital where his daughter was being cared for, the staff soon noticed that the little girl was clutching onto the squid's tentacles rather than all the wires and tubes inside the incubator, and that she seemed calmer and more secure.

Soon afterwards, two volunteers named Jeanette Bøgelund Bentzen and Mia Clement started crocheting squids for the neonatal units at three hospitals. Just nine days later, the Danish Octo Project was born. Today it has around seventeen ambassadors (not to mention countless octopi!), and word of the group's history and work has spread overseas. There are now Octo groups in a host of countries around the world, including Sweden, the UK, France, Spain, Luxembourg, Holland, Belgium, Romania, Argentina and Canada.

All members of the group – including the main coordinators, ambassadors and webmasters – are volunteers, individuals with a burning desire to make a difference to the lives of premature babies and their families. As well as the core group itself, volunteers crochet and knit cute squids and jellyfish before sending them to the ambassadors.

The group's work consists of collecting and then washing and packing the Octos before delivering them to neonatal units. A stay at a neonatal unit is often long, and marked with progress and setbacks. A playful, colourful Octo can bring vibrancy to a harsh, clinical incubator and give some much-needed encouragement to the baby's family.

Over twenty-
two thousand
Octos have
already been
donated to
hospitals
across
Denmark.

I DAG ER JEG
1 UGE
GAMMEL

Why newborns love Octos

Most newborns will benefit from having their subconscious nervous system soothed – and that goes for both full-term babies and premature births. The subconscious nervous system controls their blood pressure, heart rate, and breathing and digestion, so it's essential to their survival.

Premature babies in particular often experience stress or pressure on this system and need soothing. This is often attributed to their senses being more delicate, because they're not 'fully baked'. Not only that, these babies are often exposed to unpleasant stimuli, such as bleeping monitors, and necessary but painful procedures such as blood tests. These children are often unable to experience skin-to-skin contact with mum or dad, something that is usually both comforting and calming.

We can help these newborns by stimulating and soothing their nervous systems, and in this way we can steer the nervous system into regulating itself more appropriately. That's why it is useful to know about our three primary senses:

1 The vestibular sense – works a little bit like a spirit level. It is located within the inner ear and registers any head movements. There are three semi-circular canals, each stimulated by turning, jumping and swinging movements respectively.

2 Proprioception – found in all our muscles and joints. This sense registers movement throughout the body – whether we are bending or extending a joint – what force we are using and determines the body's position in space.

3 Touch – a sense felt all over our skin and in mucus membranes. It registers temperature, pressure, pain and contact. We use this sense to 'feel the world' and it helps us, among other things, to determine what is dangerous for the body to touch, and what isn't.

By stimulating these three senses we are able to help the baby's subconscious nervous system regulate itself. This in turn can lead to improvements in blood pressure, heart rate, breathing and digestion, which become calmer and more restful, helping to improve well-being.

'When the Octo is placed alongside the baby, it feels like the baby is touching something solid, like the internal wall of mum's comforting womb. This stimulates both proprioception and the sense of touch, and the baby becomes calmer. Similarly, these senses are activated when the child grasps one of the Octo's tentacles. The Octo's curly tentacle feels like the umbilical cord, which makes it seem familiar. This calms the nervous system still further and improves the child's well-being.'

Kit Bak and Mette Degn Larsen

Kit Bak and Mette Degn Larsen
Child Physiotherapist, Psychotherapist.
Both work with children's ability to pick up, co-ordinate and react appropriately to sensory stimulation.

The world's best Octos!

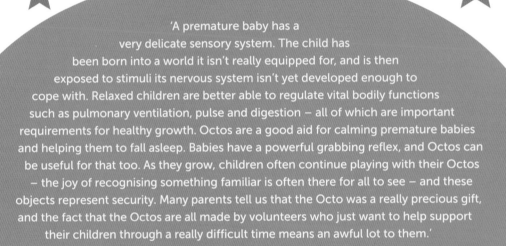

'A premature baby has a very delicate sensory system. The child has been born into a world it isn't really equipped for, and is then exposed to stimuli its nervous system isn't yet developed enough to cope with. Relaxed children are better able to regulate vital bodily functions such as pulmonary ventilation, pulse and digestion – all of which are important requirements for healthy growth. Octos are a good aid for calming premature babies and helping them to fall asleep. Babies have a powerful grabbing reflex, and Octos can be useful for that too. As they grow, children often continue playing with their Octos – the joy of recognising something familiar is often there for all to see – and these objects represent security. Many parents tell us that the Octo was a really precious gift, and the fact that the Octos are all made by volunteers who just want to help support their children through a really difficult time means an awful lot to them.'

Jannie Haaber
NIDCAP Professional, Registered Nurse, Neonatal Clinic at
Rigshospitalet Copenhagen.

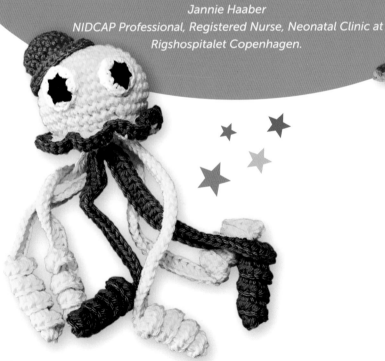

'We were suddenly, far too early, about to become parents. We were a long way from home — and we had arrived there without any of our things. Since we hadn't brought any cuddly toys for our little boy, it really meant a lot to us when we were given an Octo to keep him company. It changed the feel of the incubator — it didn't feel as cold, and that was a little ray of light in a difficult, unfamiliar situation. We're so glad that his first cuddly toy ended up being an Octo. It's now his most faithful companion!'

Louise Schultz
Parent

'My son was born at full-term in March 1997, but he still needed to spend time in intensive care at the neonatal clinic during the first ten days of his life. It's quite a shocking experience to see your new-born child fighting for his life, with all those tubes and machines all over the place, but we found it really moving when he was given a little handmade bonnet. Just the thought of a complete stranger giving of their time to send us a little bit of love, without so much as a thank you for their selfless efforts. When I read Josefine's blog entry about the father who was trying to find a crocheted little octopus for his premature daughter Sofia, I'd been thinking about doing something for premature babies for a while. I started collecting crocheted Octos for the families at Odense University Hospital's Neonatal Unit. That was the start of what later became the Danish Octo Project — the idea of it was that parents of premature babies all over Denmark might experience a little ray of light from an unexpected source.'

Mia Clément, founding member of
the Danish Octo Project

11

Before you start...

CROCHET NEEDLE

For the crocheted Octos you will need a crochet needle size B – E. If the needle doesn't suit your tension, you can use a slightly smaller or slightly larger size.

If you do a lot of crocheting, it's worth choosing a good, ergonomic needle, one with a comfortable grip that's kinder to your hands.

YARN

Only ever use 100% cotton yarn. The best yarns for Octos and jellyfish are those with a simple thread, e.g. 4ply or 8ply cotton, both of which have a lovely soft quality. Crochet tension varies a lot from one person to another, so the thickness of the thread should suit your style. An infinite number of variations are possible, both in terms of the size and appearance of your Octos. Of course it's fine to use left-over yarn – as long as it's pure cotton. Using multi-coloured leftovers can give your Octos their own unique expression, and colourful Octos are always popular!

FILLING

It's really important that the Octos can be washed, so the best filling is something like soft toy stuffing or other material that can be washed at 60°C. You could also use the filler from a cheap pillow.

Don't be tempted to use leftover yarn or ordinary cotton wool – both really disintegrate in the wash. Remember to get the Octos really well stuffed, because the stuffing will settle a bit after the first wash.

EYES

For safety reasons, you should only crochet or embroider your Octos' eyes. Do not use buttons or sew-on eyes.

You can crochet or embroider all kinds of funny eyes on your Octo. You'll find the instructions for making eyes on pages 24 & 25, but feel free to be inspired by all the Octos featured in this book!

MAGIC RING

The process of making both Octos and jellyfish starts with a 'Magic Ring'. See how to make one on page 14. There are also plenty of videos online that show you how it's done. Once you've done it a couple of times there'll be no stopping you!

ABBREVIATIONS:

MR = Magic Ring

rd = round

st = stitch

dc = double crochet

ch = chain

tog = together

sl st = slip stitch

htr = half treble

tr = treble

* = this step should be repeated

(Uses UK terminology)

Crochet school!

THE MAGIC RING

1 Place the yarn as shown here. It should form a loop resting on your index finger.

2 Pinch thumb and index finger together at the point where the thread crosses itself.

3 Push the needle through the loop. Wrap the yarn over the needle, and then pull the loop closed.

4 Holding the loop tightly, wrap the yarn over the needle and pull the thread through the stitch on the needle.

5 Now you can crochet the six stitches that will make up the ring. Pull carefully on the end of the yarn to pull the ring tighter.

6 Once you've crocheted the whole thing together you can keep working from those six stiches.

SLIP STITCH

1 Place the needle inside the first stitch, and wrap the yarn around the needle. Then pull the needle through both stiches.

2 Pull the yarn through.

3 Keep working through the stitches with the needle.

DOUBLE CROCHET

1 Push the needle through the first stitch. Pull it through both loops.

2 Yarn over.

3 Pull the yarn through. Now you have two stitches!

4 Yarn over, pull it through both stitches.

5 Finished!

HALF TREBLE CROCHET

1 Yarn over.

2 Pick the yarn through the first, so you have three stitches on the needle.

3 Yarn over, then pull it through all three stitches.

TREBLE CROCHET

1 Follow steps 1 and 2 of the half treble crochet.

2 Yarn over, then pull it through the first two stitches.

3 Yarn over, then pull it through the last two stitches.

How to crochet an Octo

Start off by making a Magic Ring. You'll find the instructions on page 14.

Rd 1: 6 dc in the ring.

Rd 2: *2 dc in each stitch*, rep x 6 = 12 sts

Rd 3: *2 dc in first st, 1 dc in next st*, rep x 6 = 18 sts

Rd 4: *2 dc in first st, 1 dc in next 2 st*, rep x 6 = 24 sts

Rd 5: *2 dc in first st, 1 dc in next 3 st*, rep x 6 = 30 sts

Rd 6: *2 dc in first st, 1 dc in next 4 st*, rep x 6 = 36 sts

Rd 7–14: 1 dc in each st = 36 sts in each round

Rd 15: *dc decrease, 1 dc in next 4 st*, rep x 6 = 30 sts

Rd 16–17: 1 dc in each st = 30 st

Rd 18: *dc decrease, 1 dc in next 3 st*, rep x 6 = 24 sts

Rd 19–20: 1 dc in each st = 24 st

Rd 21: *dc decrease, 1 dc in next 2 st*, rep x 6 = 18 sts

Rd 22: 1 dc in each st = 18 st

Rd 23: *dc decrease, 1 dc in next 7 st*, rep x 2 = 16 sts

Rd 24: 1 dc in each st = 16 st

Rd 25: this is where the tentacles start. They are crocheted straight onto the head, and there are eight of them: 1 dc, 50 ch, turn and crochet 2 dc in each ch, finishing with a dc*.

Repeat the tentacle process seven times. Finish with a sl st in the last stich, then push the thread through. (If you're struggling to get the tentacles to curl nicely, you can crochet three or four dc in each ch instead.)

IMPORTANT! The tentacles must not be longer than 22cm at full stretch, to avoid becoming a choking hazard. If they end up being too long, just remove a few chains.

BASE

Rd 1: 5 dc in a Magic Ring

Rd 2: 2 dc in each st = 10 sts

Rd 3: *2 dc in first st, 1 dc in next st*, rep x 5 = 15 sts. Finish with a sl st and sew in the end.

ASSEMBLY

Using the stuffing material of your choice, stuff the Octo's body and then sew the base onto it. Attach or embroider the eyes, and sew on a mouth using your preferred stitch, e.g. a slip stitch.

How to make a crocheted jellyfish

BODY

Start by making a Magic Ring. You'll find the instructions on page 14.

Rd 1: 6 dc in the ring

Rd 2: *2 dc in each stitch*, rep x 6= 12 sts

Rd 3: *2 dc in first st, 1 dc in next st*, rep x 6 = 18 sts

Rd 4: *2 dc in first st, 1 dc in next 2 st*, rep x 6 = 24 sts

Rd 5: *2 dc in first st, 1 dc in next 3 st*, rep x 6 = 30 sts

Rd 6: *2 dc in first st, 1 dc in next 4 st*, rep x 6 = 36 sts

Rd 7–11: 1 dc in every dc = 36 st

Rd 12: *dc decrease, 1 dc in next 4 st*, rep x 6 = 30 sts

Rd 13: *dc decrease, 1 dc in next 3 st*, rep x 6 = 24 sts

Now it's time for the crown. Turn the front of the piece towards you, so that you're crocheting in the front loop only.

Rd 14: in front loop, crochet 5 tr in the same dc, skip one dc, 1 sl st in the next dc* *-* repeat until you have 8 arch stitches. In the last of the arches (the eighth), crochet 5 tr in the same dc, then 1 sl st in the next dc (i.e. don't skip a dc as in the previous seven arches). You are now working in both stitches again.

Rd 15: crochet *1 dc, 2 dc in that same dc, 1 dc, 2 dc inside that same dc, 1 dc and 1 dc in the sl st from the last round. *-* = repeat for each bow.

Finish off with a sl st in the dc closest to the start of the round. Fasten off the ends.

BASE

Make a Magic Ring

Rd 1: 6 dc in the ring

Rd 2: 2 dc in each dc = 12 st

Rd 3: *2 dc in first st, 1 dc in next st*, rep x 6 = 18 sts

Rd 4: *2 dc in first st, 1 dc in next 2 st*, rep x 6 = 24 sts

ASSEMBLY

Now sew the base onto the body. You can also crochet it onto the back loops left free after round 14.

Now stuff the jellyfish with stuffing material before sewing it up.

TENTACLES

The six tentacles are crocheted straight onto the base of the jellyfish. Don't worry too much about where they attach to

the base. Start by putting the first arm anywhere on the base.

Each tentacle has 45 ch. Starting with the second ch from the the needle, crochet two htr in each of the first eight ch. From there on, crochet one htr in each ch. When you reach the base again, finish the tentacle off by crocheting it into the base at the same place where you started from. That will make sure it's securely attached. Crochet 1 dc into the base between each tentacle. Crochet the remaining tentacles in the same way. Weave in the ends.

How to Knit an Octo

ABBREVIATIONS

k = knit stitch

k2tog = knit 2 stitches together (decrease)

increase = knit 2 stitches in 1 stitch

Knit new stitches around the outside (for the tentacles)

slip a stitch = move the stitch onto the right needle without knitting it. But remember it still counts!

YOU WILL NEED

Pair of 2.75mm (UK size 12) knitting needles

100% cotton yarn – simple thread, 4ply cotton yarn or no. 3 crochet cotton

BEFORE YOU START

You're going to knit the Octo lengthways with two needles (or back and forth on a circular needle), and then sew the whole thing together.

All stitches are knitted flat.

The technique used is called *short rows* or *turning rows*. In this method, you turn the piece around and then knit back in the opposite direction before the row is finished. Shifting the point at which you turn gives the shape of the piece (see the illustration on page 22). Before finishing a tentacle, make sure that there are 22 stitches back to the body. Each time you turn around without knitting the whole row, it's a good idea to start by slipping a stitch (move the stitch onto the right needle without knitting it) – but don't forget to count it!

BODY AND TENTACLES

Cast on 22 stitches.

Row 1: k22, cast on 40 st, turn. (62 st)

Row 2: k60, turn.

Row 3: k18, turn.

Row 4: k16, turn.

Row 5: k14, turn.

Row 6: k13, turn.

Row 7: k11, turn.

Row 8: k9, turn.

Row 9: knit to the tentacle (15 st), continue into the tentacle, increasing as follows:

Knit 1 st in the top loop without removing it from the left needle, yarn over needle, then knit 1 st in the bottom loop (see pictures on pages 22 and 23).

Repeat for all 40 st, turn.

Row 10: Finish the tentacle. Now k22 on the needle back to the body.

Row 11: k22, yarn over needle back to tentacle number 2. Repeat rows 2 to 11, 8 times in total (Octos have eight tentacles)

BASE

Next row: k3, yarn over needle.
Next row: knit. **Next row:** increase 1
st, k3. (5 st) **Next row:** knit. **Next row:**
increase 1 st, k5. (7 st) **Next row:** knit.
Next row: k2tog in first 2 st and last 2 st.
(5 st) **Next row:** knit. **Next row:** k2tog in
first 2 st and last 2 st. (3 st) Cast off.

ASSEMBLY

Sew the Octo together through the
outermost row of stitches. Pull a thread
through the outermost row of stitches
at the top, push through and tie off.
Stuff the Octo's body, then sew it onto
the base.

WRAP AND TURN

First knit 22 flat stitches, then knit 40 stitches and turn.

Knit 60 flat stitches back the other way, turning when there are two stitches left.

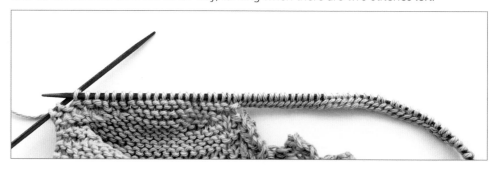

When you turn, remember to slip stitch knitwise with yarn in front. After that, knit 18 flat stitches and turn. Keep repeating (see diagram below).

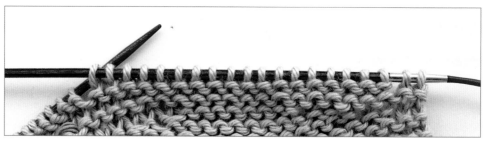

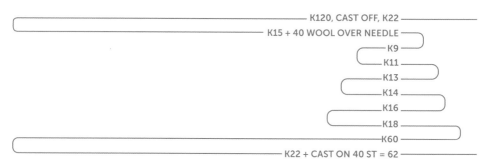

K120, CAST OFF, K22

K15 + 40 WOOL OVER NEEDLE

K9

K11

K13

K14

K16

K18

K60

K22 + CAST ON 40 ST = 62

SLIP STITCH

Move the stitch over to the right-hand needle without knitting it. Remember to count it, though!

INCREASE WITH YARN OVER NEEDLE

Knit one stitch in the innermost loop without taking it off the left-hand needle, yarn over and knit one stitch in the outermost loop. Repeat for all 40 stitches.

Faces

A face, especially if it's one with a funny or strange expression, can really bring an Octo to life. The possibilities are endless, and often this is the most fun part of the process – giving the Octos life and their own characteristics. Here are a few tips on how to give your Octo a face. There are, of course, countless alternatives – and what your Octo looks like is all down to you!

EMBROIDERED EYES

The easiest way to put eyes on your Octo is to embroider them. Thread a darning needle with your chosen colour, making sure to tie the end securely. Once you've done that, you can experiment with all sorts of different kinds of eyes.

CROCHETED EYES

You can crochet eyes onto your Octo. They take time to make, but it isn't difficult, and you can choose the size and colour of the eyes – whatever takes your fancy!

Start with white yarn.
Rd 1: 5 dc in a Magic Ring = 5 st
Rd 2: 2 dc in every st, all the way round = 10 st
Tie off a long end. You can use this to sew the eye on later. You could also make it a little reflection in the pupil.

The pupil is made from black yarn.
Rd 1: 4 dc in a Magic Ring
Tie off a long end. You'll use this to sew the pupil into position. You can also use it to embroider a little eyebrow.

Sew the white of the eye onto the Octo. Use the end of the pupil-yarn to make, for example, a little eyebrow or a mouth. Attach the end securely.
You might want to use the white end to knit a discreet little white line inside the pupil – and give your Octo a real twinkle in its eye!

Other accessories and decorations

BASIC METHOD FOR MAKING AN OCTO-CAP

You can also give your Octo extra personality by making it a hat. Caps are easy to make.
They follow the same basic principle as the Octo itself, but with a number of stitches
greater than 36. A hat can be any colour, and when it comes to helmets, the only limit is
your imagination. A bicycle helmet, a soldier's helmet, a hard hat – keep experimenting,
and just enjoy being creative along the way!

MAKE A HELMET

Rd 1: 6 dc in an MR = 6 st

Rd 2: *2 dc in each st* repeat 6 times = 12 st

Rd 3: *2 dc in first st, 1 dc in next st*, repeat 6 times = 18 st

Rd 4: *2 dc in first st, 1 dc in next 2 st*, repeat 6 times = 24 st

Rd 5: *2 dc in first st, 1 dc in next 3 st*, repeat 6 times = 30 st

Rd 6: *2 dc in first st, 1 dc in next 4 st*, repeat 6 times = 36 st

Rd 7: *2 dc in first st, 1 dc in next 5 st*, repeat 6 times = 42 st

Rd 8: *1 dc in each st all the way round

Repeat rd 8 until it looks like the hat/ helmet is about the right size for your Octo. It's a good idea to leave a long tail when fastening off. You can then use this to sew the hat firmly onto the Octo's head to make sure it doesn't come off.

MAKING A CHINSTRAP

There are lots of great ways to make a chinstrap for your helmet. The most important thing, though, is that it is really well attached so that it can't come loose and get tangled around tiny fingers or hospital equipment.

HOW IT'S DONE

1 Choose a stitch on the last round of the helmet, then stitch a slip stitch, giving you a starting point for your strap. The helmet in the picture has a strap starting from where the helmet is fastened off, so the fastening off for the strap itself is on the back of the Octo.

2 Crochet a long row of ch, until you think the strap is the right length. You can try the hat on the Octo to give yourself an idea. Everyone crochets differently, so the number of ch you'll need will vary according to how tight you crochet your stitches.

3 Crochet the strap onto a stitch in the helmet's last round using a slip stitch. It's completely up to you where the strap starts and finishes. Fasten off, leaving a good long tail.

4 The long tail is then used to attach the strap firmly to the Octo. Remember to weave in the end where the strap starts too, so that baby's fingers can't grab hold of it.

TOP HAT

Each round is fastened off with 1 sl st in the round's first dc to allow the next round to attach, because the hat shape isn't crocheted in a spiral, unlike Octos.

MAKING THE TOP OF THE HAT

Rd 1: 6 dc in an MR = 6 st

Rd 2: *2 dc in each st* repeat 6 times = 12 st

Rd 3: *2 dc in first st, 1 dc in next st* repeat 6 times = 18st

Rd 4: crochet 1 ch after each of the previous rd. Turn the work around, so that you have the wrong side up. Now crochet 1 sl st in each st all the way around the edge. This turned-down edge on the top's wrong side will let you crochet downwards = 18 st.

MAKING THE HAT CYLINDER

Rd 5: 1 dc in each st of the turned down edge from rd 4 = 18 st

Rd 6–9: 1 dc in each st. Each rd ends with a sl st in the round's first st and a ch to start the next rd.

MAKING THE HAT BAND

Change colour

Rd 10: crochet 1 htr in each st all the way around.

Rd 11: 1 dc in each st all the way around.

MAKING THE HAT BRIM

Change yarn, back to the hat's original colour.

Rd 12: crochet 1 dc in each st all the way round the bottom of the hat band. This is your base for crocheting the hat's brim. Finish with a sl st in the first sl st and then a ch.

Rd 13 is worked into the sl st from rd 13. *2 dc in the first sl st, 1 dc in each of the next 2 sl st*, repeat 6 times = 24 st

Rd 14: *2 dc in first st, 1 dc in each of the next 3 st*, repeat 6 times = 30 st

Fasten off with a long tail, which can be used to attach the hat onto the Octo.

Stuff your top hat using the same material that you used to stuff your Octo.

OCTO-HAIR
– WORN UP, IN A BUN

Rd 1: (hair) start with 6 dc in an MR

Rd 2: 2 dc in each st = 12 st

Rd 3: *2 dc in first st, 1 dc in next st* Repeat 6 times = 18 st

Rd 4: 1 dc in each st all the way round = 18 st

Rd 5: *dc decrease, 1 dc in next st*, repeat six times = 12 st

Rd 6: *dc decrease*, repeat 6 times = 6 st Stuff the bun.

Rd 7: Now follow the instructions from **How to crochet an Octo** rd 2–10:

Rd 8: *2 dc in each stitch* rep x 6 = 12 sts

Rd 9: *2 dc in first st, 1 dc in next st*, rep x 6 = 18 sts

Rd 10: *2 dc in first st, 1 dc in next 2 st*, rep x 6 = 24 sts

Rd 11: *2 dc in first st, 1 dc in next 3 st*, rep x 6 = 30 sts

Rd 12: *2 dc in first st, 1 dc in next 4 st*, rep x 6 = 36 sts

Rd 13–15: 1 dc in each st all the way round = 36 st

Change yarn, to the main colour of your Octo.

Rd 16–19: 1 dc in each st all the way round = 36 st

Rd 20: *4 dc, 1 dc decrease* 6 times in total = 30 st

Rd 21–22: 1 dc in each st all the way round = 30 st

Rd 23: *3 dc, 1 dc decrease* 6 times in total = 24 st

Rd 24–25: 1 dc in each st all the way round = 24 st

Rd 26: *2 dc, 1 dc decrease* 6 times in total = 18 st

Rd 27: 1 dc in each st all the way round = 18 st

Rd 28: 1 dc decrease, 7 dc, 1 dc decrease, 7 dc = 16 st

You can even make a little hairband using chain stitches that can be placed around the bun. Remember to attach it securely.

HAIRBAND WITH FLORAL DECORATION

Work a slip stitch into a stitch at the top of the Octo, using the colour you would like to use for your hairband. Work sl st all the way around the round you have chosen to follow on the Octo, as shown in the picture. Pull a good length of yarn right through the last sl st.

LITTLE GREEN LEAF

Crochet 5 ch for the long side. Then work a sl st into the second st from the needle. 1 dc in the next st. 1 htr in the next st. 1 sl st in the last ch. Pull the rest of the yarn right through the stitch, and weave in the end securely. Sew the loose end into the inside of the Octo.

LITTLE FLOWER

The first ch forms the centre of the flower, so the petals are crocheted outwards starting from that first ch.
Work 3 ch in the colour you have chosen for the flower.
Then work 1 htr through the first ch, 1 sl st in first ch. This is the first petal. Continue working 2 ch, 1 htr and one sl st for each petal. Make 3 or 4 petals.

WOOLLY HAT

A woolly hat is a great way to use up any leftover yarn. Have fun experimenting with different colours and techniques.

HOW IT'S DONE

Rd 1: 6 dc in a MR = 6 st

Rd 2: *2 dc in each st*, repeat 6 times = 12 st

Rd 3: *2 dc in first st, 1 dc in next st*, repeat 6 times = 18 st

Rd 4: *2 dc in first st, 1 dc in next 2 st*, repeat 6 times = 24 st

Rd 5: *2 dc in first st, 1 dc in next 3 st*, repeat 6 times = 30 st

Rd 6: *2 dc in first st, 1 dc in next 4 st*, repeat 6 times = 36 st

Rd 7: *2 dc in first st, 1 dc in next 5 st*, repeat 6 times = 42 st

Rd 8–16: 1 dc in each st all the way around.

Rd 17: 1 dc in each of the first 10 st. Then work 7 tr at the end furthest from the needle. 1 dc in each of the nearest 3 st. 1 ch in next st.

BRIM OF THE HAT

Crochet front loop only: 1 dc in next st.
1 htr in next st. 1 tr in next 2 st. 2 tr in next
st. 1 tr in next 5 st. 2 tr in next st. 1 tr in
next 2 st. 1 htr in next st. 1 dc in next st.
Crochet through both loops again: 1 dc
in next st. 1 dc in next 4 dc. Work 7 tr
in the second st away from the needle.
Crochet 1 dc in the second st away from
the needle.

Fasten off with a long tail. You can use it
to sew the hat firmly onto the Octo.

Octo-tips!

FILLING

It's important not to crochet your Octo too loosely, since that might let the filling fall out. The stitches should remain tight even after the filling has been inserted.

TENTACLES

The secret to getting nice uniform tentacles is down to how you hold them while you're crocheting. To make the tentacles curl in a uniform way, you need to hold the Octo in such a way that they are free to curl up, with no obstructions. On the other hand, it doesn't really matter if they don't go curly – as long as there's something to hold on to.

For the most premature babies, it's actually a good thing if the tentacles aren't too curly, because this can make them thicker and difficult for tiny hands to grasp.

For safety reasons, it's important that the tentacles do not exceed 22 centimetres when fully extended.

There are lots of online tutorials that can show you how to make fantastic curly tentacles.

WASHING

If you're making an Octo for a child you know, you should wash it before use. Machine wash at 60°C, preferably with hypoallergenic washing powder.

Can I make Octos for the Danish Octo Project?

If you'd like to donate Octos to premature babies it's important to do so through one of the Danish Octo Project's ambassadors, since hospitals don't have the resources to deal with too many enquiries from the public. One condition that hospitals always insist upon when accepting donated Octos is that they arrive via the Danish Octo Project ambassadors. You can find the names and contact details of ambassadors via spruttegruppen.dk. There are a few other things you will need to bear in mind:

MATERIALS

Neonatal clinics only accept Octos made from either 100% cotton or bamboo yarn – acrylics can shed small fibres that can get into babies' eyes and mouths.

WHAT SIZE SHOULD MY OCTOS BE?

Octos are welcome in all shapes and sizes, but those intended for premature babies shouldn't be too large, since many of these babies are surrounded by lots of equipment, and that doesn't leave a lot of room in the incubator. A length of between 14 to 17cm including tentacles is about right.

SHOULD I WASH MY OCTO?

The ambassadors wash all the Octos with hypoallergenic washing powder before sealing them, one by one, into cellophane bags. So don't worry about washing them before you pass them on to the ambassadors.

Read more: spruttegruppen.dk or facebook.com/spruttegruppen

Thanks

This book would never have become a reality without the help of a whole host of very dedicated individuals.

Big thanks to:

Ditte Fischer, Tina Hougaard Friis, Mia Clément, Jeanette Bøgelund, Josefine Hagen Solgaard, Signe Damtoft Siersbæk, Jannie Haaber, Kit Bak, Mette Degn Larsen, Louise Schultz, Laura Linder, Aleksandra Szymaniec, Line Thomsen, Mikala Skou, Marziyeh Elahi, Kirsten Høholt, Kirstine Dalsgaard Larsen, Michelle and Kenny Højlund Tang, Mia and Mikkel Carlseng, Cecilie and Ulrik Grønbjerg Vej-Hansen.

The models:
Lilian, Valdemar, Samuel, Nikolaj, Ellen, Gry, Arn and Stella.

And of course a big thanks to everyone who made all the Octos and Jellyfish that appear on these pages!